Electronic Journal Literature

Electronic

Journal

Literature

IMPLICATIONS FOR SCHOLARS
Jan Olsen

Mecklermedia
Westport • London

Library of Congress Cataloging-in-Publication Data

Olsen, Jan.
    Electronic journal literature : implications for scholars / Jan
Olsen.
        p. cm.
    Includes bibliographical references and index.
    ISBN 0-88736-925-1 : $
    1. Electronic journals–United States. 2. Learning and
scholarship–United States. 3. Magazine design. 4. User interfaces
(Computer systems) I. Title.
PN4878.1.047 1994
050'.285–dc20   93-6314
                                                                      CIP

British Library Cataloguing-in-Publication Data

Olsen, Jan
    Electronic Journal Literature:
    Implications for Scholars
    I. Title
    070.5

    ISBN 0-88736-925-1

Mecklermedia Corporation, 11 Ferry Lane West, Westport, CT 06880.
Mecklermedia Ltd., Artillery House, Artillery Row, London SW1P 1RT, U.K.

Printed on acid free paper.
Printed and bound in the United States of America.

CONTENTS

▌List of Tables

1
INTRODUCTION

K nowledge is an unusually powerful commodity. It provides the basis for innovative solutions to society's problems and the resources for an informed citizenry. It is key to the progress of a society.

The knowledge wealth of this nation is dependent not only on the generation of new knowledge, but also, just as important, on the communication of it between the nation's scholars. Academic productivity is heavily dependent upon this communication process, and a considerable portion of the training of a scholar is directed toward learning its mechanics.

Communication involves both formal and informal methods.[1] The informal domain includes communications such as conference presentations and conversations with colleagues. This is not meant to have the same attributes as formal communication which occurs through the scholarly journal literature. In the informal domain, the information is considered unfinished, not yet reliable. On the other hand, the information presented through the journal literature receives the widest possible exposure to critical evaluation and is examined within the broadest context of knowledge. It is only here that a research result becomes eligible for status as a "finding."

The publishing of journal literature is a vast enterprise in the United States. The importance of the journal is well illustrated by the fact that, although commercial publishing houses produce a high percentage of journals, some of the most important and prestigious are produced by national, professional associations of scholars. In fact, the very first scholarly journal ever published was the *Philosophical Transactions* of the Royal Society of London in 1665.[2]

The scholars are adamant about the importance to them of journal literature:

It's life and death. It's essential. – Chemist
Absolutely I can't do without it. – Humanist
Heavens, I use it every day. – Sociologist

Traditionally, publication of knowledge has been based in the print format. Today, however, publications are being produced by the computer and stored in electronic form. Increasingly as we move through the 21st century, this technology will be a dominant means of storing and presenting scholarly information. The capabilities provided by electronic information technology for manipulating and transmitting information infuse information with a new power and a new level of significance. Societies are shifting from information in traditional print format to information in electronic form. In its report, *Global Competition: The New Reality* (1985), the President's Commission on Industrial Competitiveness concluded that success in international trade strongly depends on science, technology, and the control of information.[3]

The production of journal literature is not escaping the computer revolution. Publishers are beginning to replace the paper medium by the electronic presentation of journals.[4] Journal text is available through online access from vendors or publishers such as BRS Information Technologies, Dialog Information Services Inc., and the American Chemical Society; or on compact discs from UMI (University Microfilms International), Chadwyck-Healey Inc., and some national, professional associations such as the American Society of Agronomy. New journals are being created, electronic from their outset, and distributed via the NREN. The nation is abuzz with conferences, workshops, and list serve exchanges concerned with the latest developments of the "e-journal." Large-scale collaborative projects are under way by publishers, academe, and industry to further the state of electronic journals.[5]

The major fascination with the concept of the electronic journal is driven by several ideas: the electronic publishing process will be quicker in disseminating research findings than the production cycle of the printed journal; the electronic journal stores in a small space; large bodies of electronic text can be searched in complex ways not possible manually with the print equivalent; and electronic journals can be accessed at the user's convenience.

These efficiencies are important since they overcome some of the most significant deficiencies of the printed form of journal literature. In large research universities, for example, the case is being made that electronic journals can be accessed by the scholar at his or her microcomputer workstation, and allow much more rapid retrieval of information from the vast corpus of text than when that text is stored in print. It is also argued that the electronic form of journals saves the large amounts of space required by printed journals and solves the problem of the deterioration of paper volumes.

There is little argument that the computer can change the way in which tasks are done. For the user, however, the transfer from print to screen is not a simple process. The act of reading literary text on a screen rather than in print is not just a matter of computer performance but, more important, is a matter of human performance. For example, readers find that their ability to identify and comprehend the required information is impaired by the presentation of the text on the screen. In addition, reading from a computer screen is slower and more fatiguing than reading the printed page. In general, readers find literary text presented on a screen difficult to use.[6]

Given these conditions, it is conceivable that journal literature in electronic form could disenfranchise the reader. Such an outcome is unacceptable, given the critical role of journal literature in scholars' communication and research processes.

The study presented in this book was compelled by the concern that if journals are to be electronic, it is important that they should be structured to accommodate not only the physical tasks carried out by scholars, but also the human experience at stake.

It is critical, then, to know how scholars use journal literature. The broad question is, "What are the particular processes carried out by scholars with journal literature which are so fundamental to scholarship that they must be accommodated by the electronic version of journals?" This study identifies those processes. The intent is to make clear for systems and interface designers what is at stake for the scholar when journal literature is not in the traditional printed form, but is stored in computerized form, searched using software, and presented for reading on a computer screen. The fundamental issue is that journal literature in electronic form should not be counter-productive to the scholar's academic work.

The findings of the study have been synthesized to answer the question, "What are significant concerns in designing the electronic journal?" The study's conclusions indicate that the interaction between scholars and the text of journal literature is very different from the interaction between users and other types of text. For the scholar, it is often not a matter of setting out to locate definable information, but rather entering an extensive knowledge environment and casting around for "an intellectual adventure of some sort."

The purpose and nature of the interaction between scholar and scholarly text is quite different from that between a user and other genres of text such as legal cases, newspapers, annual reports, fiction, etc. This represents the key difference between the way information is sought and found in journal literature and the way it is sought and found by users of other types of text. This is significant since the process is intrinsic to the scholars' real purposes in using journal literature—creative thinking, learning, and analytical thinking.

If electronic journals are to be structured to support scholars' effective interaction with the literature, then two major design problems must be solved. The first is to allow human, not computer recognition to make the optimal "connections" with the literature, and the second is to support the scholars' reading styles and visual comfort.

The intent of this study is captured in the words of Wittgenstein: "I wouldn't dream of trying to drive anyone out of this paradise. I would do something quite different; I would try to show you that it is not a paradise."[7]

—— Notes ——

1. William D. Garvey, *Communication: The Essence of Science* (New York: Pergamon Press, 1979), 143–45.
2. A. J. Meadows, ed., *The Scientific Journal* (London: Aslib, 1979), 9.
3. U.S. President's Commission on Industrial Competitiveness, *Global Competition: The New Reality*, Vol. 1 (Washington, D.C.: United States Government Printing Office, 1985).
4. Lorrin R. Garson and Stanley M. Cohen, *Users' Manual: Primary Journal Database, ACS Full-Text File* (Washington, DC: American Chemical Society, 1983); Alexander C. Hoffman, "Electro-copying and Collective Administration of Rights," *Rights* 2(1) (1988): 2, 11–12; William J. Broad, "Journals: Fearing the Electronic Future," *Science* 216 (28 May 1982): 964–68.

5. Michael Lesk, "The CORE Electronic Chemistry Library," in *Proceedings of the Fourteenth Annual International ACM/SIGIR Conference on Research and Development in Information Retrieval,* Chicago, 13–16 Oct. 1991 (New York: Association for Computing Machinery), 93–112; Richard Lucier, Robert Badger, Ed Szurkowski, and Guy Story, paper presented at ARL/CAUSE/EDUCOM Coalition for Networked Information, Nov. 19–20, 1992 Meeting of the Task Force.
6. Patricia Wright, "Reading and Writing for Electronic Journals," in *Executive Control Processes in Reading,* eds. Bruce K. Britton and Shawn M. Glynn (Hillsdale, NJ: Lawrence Erlbaum Associates, Publishers, 1987), 23–52; Edward Barrett, ed., *Text, Context, and HyperText: Writing With and For the Computer* (Cambridge, MA: MIT Press, 1988); David H. Jonassen, ed., *The Technology of Text* (Englewood Cliffs, NJ: Educational Technology Publications, 1982); Charles Hulme, "Reading: Extracting Information from Printed and Electronically Presented Text," in *Fundamentals of Human-Computer Interaction,* ed. Andrew Monk (New York: Academic Press, 1984), 35–47.
7. Ray Monk, *Ludwig Wittgenstein: The Duty of Genius* (London: Jonathan Cape, 1990), 416.

2
THE NATURE OF THE STUDY

This study set out to examine the interaction between the scholar and journal literature. The broad questions are: "What are the scholars' purposes in using the literature and what are the actual processes carried out by scholars with journal literature which must be accommodated by the electronic version of journals?" When these are understood, electronic journals can be designed to provide capabilities which will match the scholars' needs.

It was decided that this understanding could be reached most effectively by discussing directly with scholars their needs and habits in using journal literature. The questions used as a loose framework for the interview were worked out through a series of activities.

The first was a group of six pilot interviews with faculty, who were not part of the proposed population. The initial three interviews were structured as a conversation about the faculty members' use of journal literature. Minimal intervention was offered by the interviewer who instead encouraged the participants to talk freely about the use of journal literature in their academic work. This allowed the scholars' idiosyncratic points of view, habits, motives, and concerns to emerge. The purpose of these conversations was to develop a framework of the issues to be explored.

Consistently during these discussions, the scholars chose to describe the role of journal literature in their academic work, their habits in working with it, and the physical tasks carried out to use it. With these conversations in mind, several categories were used for the three remaining pilot interviews. The categories were as follows:

- reasons and techniques for locating journal literature
- methods of reading journal literature
- when and where journal literature is read
- which journal literature is most useful
- speculation on advantages and disadvantages of printed journal literature compared with the electronic form
- demographics of scholars

These categories were translated into a set of appropriate questions to be used in the next three of the pilot interviews. The purpose of this group of interviews was to ensure that all aspects of the scholar's interaction with, needs, and expectations of journal literature had been noted. It was also a test of whether the questions were asked in terms to which the scholars could respond with clarity. Each person interviewed spontaneously remarked that he/she had found the interview stimulating, and the topic of research interesting and important.

The population in this study is scholars in a large research university setting. This environment was chosen because the impact of creating electronic journals in place of print will be most significant to scholars in this type of institution, since journal literature is integral to their academic work and communication. The study involves scholars representing the physical sciences, social sciences, and humanities.

To conduct the study, one discipline was selected from the physical sciences (chemistry), one from the social sciences (sociology), and one from the humanities (English). In each discipline sixteen scholars were chosen. This provided a total population of forty-eight scholars. Unfortunately two interview tapes were inaudible, reducing the population to forty-six. In order to generalize the findings, the study was carried out in two major research universities, Cornell University and the University of Pennsylvania. The participants were randomly selected from listings of assistant, associate, and full professors from each of the six departments. The interviews were transcribed and coded.

The following questions formed the loose framework for the interviews.

——— Questions for Interview ———

Reasons and Techniques for Locating Journal Literature

1. How often do you use journal literature?
2. Why do you use journal literature?
3. How do you "connect" with the journal literature, i.e., know the journal literature of your field?
   e.g.: display of current journals in the library
        personal subscriptions

               receive articles, citations from colleagues
               citations in journal articles
               computer searches
               current awareness service
               bibliographies in books

4. Do you keep abreast of the literature?
5. Which method(s) seem(s) the best?

Methods of Reading Journal Literature

6. What makes you read an article or not read an article, i.e., how do you filter out which articles you want to read?
7. Do you read the entire article?
8. If you do, in what sequence do you read the parts?
9. What do you gain from doing that?
10. If you do not read the entire article, which part(s) of it do you read?
11. If you could have access to only two parts of an article, which two would they be?
12. What do you do with the information in the article as you are reading it, and after you have read it?

  e.g.: underline
       make margin notes
       make notes on paper
       photocopy parts of the full article
       put the photocopies in a personal file of articles
       put a citation to the article in a citation file
       use it in your class as a handout
       use parts of it as overhead transparencies
       put it on reserve

When and Where Journal Literature Is Read

13. Where do you read journals the most?
  e.g.: at home
       in the library
       in the office
14. Is this different depending upon whether the journal literature is a "loose" article (e.g., a preprint, reprint, or photocopy) or in "book" form?

15. When do you read journals?
    time of day or night, week, semester
16. Is this the most desirable time for reading journals?

Which Journal Literature Is Most Useful

17. Which time span of a journal is the most useful to you?
    the current calendar year
    the last three years
    the last five years
    the last ten years
    from the beginning of the journal's publication to
    the present
18. If you had to choose, would you rather have the two or three most recent years of many journals, or all the years of a few journals, or some other combination?
19. How many personal subscriptions to academic journals do you have?
20. Do you have a personal file of journal articles? If so, how is this arranged and indexed? Are you satisfied with it?

Speculation on the Advantages and Disadvantages of Printed Journal Literature Compared with the Electronic Journal

21. Describe how you feel about using journal literature on a computer screen rather than in print.
22. What are the particular advantages for you of the print form of journal literature?
23. What are the particular disadvantages for you of the print form of journal literature?
24. What do you expect would be advantages of electronic journals over print journals?
25. What do you expect would be the limitations of an electronic journal?
26. Are there any particular factors which would encourage you to use the electronic form of the journal?
27. Are there some types of journals which would be better in print than in electronic form, and are there some which would be enhanced by being stored and used electronically?

Scholar's Demographics

Name

University

Department

Sex

Professional rank

Years of research and instruction

Area of specialty

Ph.D. from

Type of student taught:
    at least half undergraduates
    mostly undergraduates
    all undergraduates
    mostly graduates

Computer Use

Please use an (X) to indicate your response.

Do you have access to a microcomputer?
Yes_____   No _____

Do you have exclusive use of a microcomputer?
Yes_____   No_____

Where do you use the microcomputer?
At home_____   At the office_____

How often do you use a microcomputer?
Routinely_____   Occasionally_____   Not at all_____

How many hours per week do you use a microcomputer?
Less than 10_____   10-20_____   20-40_____   More_____

For what applications do you use a microcomputer?
    Word processing _____
    Statistical analysis _____
    Electronic mail to colleagues: on campus _____
                                  outside campus _____
    Database management _____

Personal file management _____
Preparing tests _____
Grading tests _____
Accessing the library's online catalog _____
Searching online databases: bibliographic _____
non-bibliographic _____
Graphics _____
Other_____

What is your level of programming skill?
non-existent____
minimal____
fair____
good____
excellent____

3
JOURNAL LITERATURE IN THE ACADEMIC WORK OF SCHOLARS

T he creation and evolution of the scholarly journal is documented in a number of publications.[1] It was created as the primary form of communication among scholars and continues that function today.

The journal, as we know it , was begun by the Royal Society of London. The Fellows of the Society felt the need for the formal communication of their experiments and findings which had, until then, been discussed through personal letters. The first issue of the *Transactions* was published in London on March 6, 1665, edited by Henry Oldenburg, secretary to the society. It was a monthly publication containing new observations and original work in science. It provided book reviews, and space to publish differing scientific opinions. It became the model for all other professional academies, and although commercial publishing houses today produce the greater number of journals, the professional associations continue to publish some of the most important and prestigious.

A number of studies have examined how scholars actually use journals. These tend to be short, behavioral studies delineating the tasks scholars perform with the journals.[2]

The seminal work on the use of journals by scholars has been conducted by William D. Garvey, a psychologist who spent many years at the Center for Research in Scientific Communication of Johns Hopkins University. Garvey followed the behavior of 2,030 scholars associated with several disciplines in the physical and social sciences. His main interest was scientific communication which he defined as:

> *the full spectrum of activities associated with production,*
> *dissemination, and use of information from the time the*
> *scientist gets the idea for his research until information*
> *about the results of this research is accepted as a constituent*
> *of scientific knowledge.*[3]

This definition includes communication from the most informal discussion between two scholars to the formal aspects of communication such as journals and books.

The importance of Garvey's work to the present study is, first, that it underscores the role of journal literature as the scholars' most important means of communication. Other writing, such as that of A. J. Meadows, also asserts the central importance of journals to scholars.[4]

Second, Garvey warns that making alterations to the communication process will not effect the desired changes in scholars' behavior unless the goals of the innovation are compatible with the individual and aggregate goals of the scholarly community. An extrapolation is that should an innovation adversely affect the communication process, the process is jeopardized.[5]

Third, he concluded in working with both physical scientists and social scientists that while their gross communication and literature patterns use are similar, the similarities can mask important differences between disciplines. He warns that: "communication innovations designed for one discipline may prove inappropriate and even damaging for another."[6] The present study took the opportunity to investigate the journal use patterns by scholars in each of the broad discipline areas of the social sciences, physical sciences, and humanities.

—— The Functions of Journal Literature ——

The importance of communication through journal literature was borne out by the scholars interviewed in this study. They maintained unanimously that journal literature is "indispensable" to their academic work. They use it to keep up to date with what others are doing, to form new ideas, to gather background information for a research area, and to look up references, facts, and methods. This was true for every scholar interviewed. (See Table 1.)

	Chemists n=16	Sociologists n=16	Humanists n=14
Table 1 **Reasons for Using Journal Literature**			
To gather background knowledge on a topic	16	16	14
To maintain current awareness	16	16	14
To search for specific items	16	16	14

Chemists use journal literature constantly, describing the frequency as "daily," "frequently," "all the time," "every hour." The sociologists are a little less intense, several using the term "fairly frequently," while humanists used the term "widely variable," linking their pattern of use to non-teaching periods such as summer or semester breaks. Specifically, 62 percent of the chemists indicated that they use the literature every day, every other day, or two-three times a week, compared with 25 percent of the sociologists and no humanists. By contrast, 42 percent of the humanists indicated that their frequency of literature use is widely variable, while 19 percent of the sociologists and no chemists used the term widely variable. (See Table 2.)

This variation appears attributable to the fact that the journal literature provides the "research front" or current state of knowledge to a greater degree for the chemists than for the sociologists and the humanists. The "research front" also changes more rapidly in the sciences than in the social sciences and humanities. In addition, sociologists and humanists use book literature more than chemists.

—— Finding the Journal Literature ——

Scholars complained repeatedly that in trying to keep up to date with the literature of their discipline they are overwhelmed by the volume of publishing. They feel it is too vast for physical and intellectual management. As one scholar expressed it: "Any individual

Table 2
Frequency of Use of Journal Literature

	Chemists n=16	Sociologists n=16	Humanists n=14
Every hour	1		
Daily	7	4	
Every other day	1		
2-3 times a week	1		
All the time	2		2
Frequently	2		2
Regularly	2	6	
Every week			5
Fairly frequently		3	
Widely variable		3	5

is reading a very small part of it." The techniques for wrestling with the problem are to subscribe to several journals, and to supplement these by reading others in the library.

Every scholar has personal subscriptions to a group of journals considered to contain the most relevant publishing. These are delivered to the desktop at home or in the office, and their arrival usually stimulates the scholar to browse through them right away. Chemists subscribe to an average number of five journals, sociologists four, and humanists six. Scholars subscribe to these journals rather than read them in the library because the inconvenience of going to the library creates the risk of the journals not being read in a timely way.

> *The proximity to the library is a very serious thing. If the library were on another floor, or worse, in another building, then I would have to take at least another five journals.*

The inconvenience factor of going to the library was mentioned in one way or another as a serious problem by all the participants interviewed. Nevertheless, the personal subscriptions are supplemented by perusing a wider set of journals in the library.

This set varies from as few as four to as many as 100 titles. Chemists scan journals in the library frequently, once or twice a week. Sociologists and humanists seem to have a different sense of urgency, browsing journals in the library every two or three months or less. Specifically 87 percent of the chemists browse a set of journals regularly in the library while 93 percent of the sociologists browse irregularly as do 80 percent of the humanists. (See Table 3.)

Table 3 Methods Used to Maintain Current Awareness			
	Chemists n=16	Sociologists n=16	Humanists n=14
Personal subscriptions to journals	16	16	14
Browsing a set of journals in the library *regularly*	14	1	3
Browsing a set of journals in the library *irregularly*	2	15	11
ad hoc browsing			11
Serendipity through browsing	14	12	12
Computer searches	4	1	
"Table of Contents" service	3	3	
Students assigned to searching literature	4		
Receives/requests preprints	5	4	
Uses references from footnotes and colleagues	6	6	4
Annual Reviews & Bibliographies	1	6	4

Occasionally I will go over to read the current periodicals in the library. Even if I get six months behind in them I will at some point go through them and see what was there.
— *Humanist*

I think there are long lags when I don't keep up with it and I'm just too busy to do the reading. Every year I sort of catch up.
— *Sociologist*

My estimate is there must be 200-300 new journals coming in every week. That may be high, there may be 200. I look at more than half of those 200 journals. I look at 100 at least.
— *Chemist*

In reviewing the journals, scholars browse by author, title, footnotes, and in the case of chemists and sociologists by abstract, graphics, and captions. They stressed that this is only given meaning, however, by flipping and scanning through the pages, to gather a sense of the whole text, and to provide the serendipitous discovery of articles. They do not like reviewing the literary front simply by using the Table of Contents of journal issues.

Scholars remarked many times that reviewing current literature can be effective only if they themselves carry it out. Methods such as computerized searching of databases of recently published references on a topic, or assigning students to search the literature, do not work well (see Table 3). They explained that they alone can make the right "connections" in deciding which literature is useful, since often an unexpected article will trigger an unpredicted train of thought. Scholars were emphatic that triggering new ideas in this way is a vital function of the journal literature and restressed the need to be able to flip and scan through the pages of a cohesive corpus of literature.

Beyond keeping up with the recent literature, scholars use the retrospective literature to provide the knowledge and published work of a particular field. Generally, they are beginning a new area of research, developing a grant proposal, or preparing a manuscript. Finding the appropriate literature means searching through a vast amount of publishing.

Chemists use computerized searching as their primary technique to accomplish this. Interestingly, this ranks a distant third for sociologists, and only one humanist uses it. (See Table 4.)

Chemists search predominantly in Chemical Abstracts Online, a very large computerized database of citations to the literature of chemistry produced by the American Chemical Society. Most typically, chemists search the database using subject terms, an author's name, or the name of a compound. Within a few minutes the chemist is provided with a list of citations to journal articles and an abstract for each article.

Sociologists pursue trains of footnotes from seminal literature as their main method of gathering the publishing on a subject.

That's what I always tell students if they are looking up something. I say "Go to the most recent article you can find and read the footnotes. That will send you to a lot of articles."

This technique is also very popular with chemists and humanists.

Table 4 Methods Used to Find Background Information			
	Chemists n=16	Sociologists n=16	Humanists n=14
Browsing a set of journals in the library	7	1	
Serendipity through browsing	8	16	5
Computer Searches	12	7	1
Student assigned to literature searching	3	5	1
Uses references from footnotes and colleagues	12	16	10
Annual Reviews/ Bibliographies	1	6	10

Humanists use annual reviews and bibliographies as their primary technique for searching through the retrospective literature. Only a very few of the sociologists use these tools, and just one chemist.

If I am doing a thorough job I start with the MLA Bibliography *(Modern Language Association), the most recent edition, and go back through every year looking for articles related to the topic I am interested in.*

The humanists also commonly use sources which provide literature reviews such as *Southern Review, Antioch Review, New York Review of Books,* and the *Times Literary Supplement.*

The task of identifying the body of journal publishing on a topic is daunting in any discipline. Traditionally it has been made easier by the availability of indexes to the literature of a discipline, for example, *Chemical Abstracts, Sociological Abstracts, Science Citation Index,* and others. Where these were once available only in printed form, and somewhat tedious to use, they have been available for a number of years in computerized form. Instead of a user having to identify the literature on a topic by working laboriously through the printed indexes published for each year, he or she can request the computer to search on the topic in the entire set of indexes, and print out the references—a matter of minutes rather than days. It is noteworthy that only the chemists use computerized searching with any regularity.

The greater willingness of the chemists to use computerized searching compared with the sociologists and humanists is tied, to some extent, to the availability of computerized indexes within the discipline. For example, Chemical Abstracts Online is a sophisticated database and close to definitive in its coverage of chemistry literature. It is a significant resource produced by the prestigious American Chemical Society and is dominant in the training and academic culture of chemists. It is also available in the chemist's office. Sociologists, on the other hand, do not have one database covering all the citations to the literature for all aspects of sociology. In some subject areas of sociology there may be several such databases, and none in others. As a result, the computerized searching of citations to the literature of a topic may not even be an available technique for some sociologists and even when it is, access to the database(s) is generally not accessible from the sociologist's office. The humanists in this study who are scholars of English have one important computerized citation database produced by their professional association and considered central to the work of every scholar of English: the *MLA Bibliography* (Publications of the Modern Language Association). However, the humanists use it in print form since they have that in their offices, and do not have the necessary terminals in their offices to access the computerized form.

Poor availability and accessibility of suitable databases certainly contribute to the low use of computerized searching, but another significant reason is the scholars' dissatisfaction with the results of the searching. Once again, the scholars stressed that only they can look at literature and select what is appropriate. Two individuals summed it up this way:

> *The computer isn't half as good as the human brain, and when I'm scanning something, I often see something that triggers a different response.*
>
> *– Humanist*

> *There's another way you do a search, and you actually begin to make connections in doing the search yourself. I can instruct a computer to do some of that and it will do it faithfully depending on how the program was written, but it still won't do it the way I do it.*
>
> *– Chemist*

At the same time, the scholars are very satisfied with the computer's ability when it is used for routine searching to retrieve citations to a specific method, or the abstract of a particular reference, or to find all the articles by an author.

—— Reading Journal Literature ——

How do scholars decide to read or not read a journal article? Do they read it in sequence? Do they read it all? What do they do with it?

Scholars were asked which parts of an article they use, in addition to the author and title, to help them decide to read or not read an article. A surprisingly clear picture emerged. (See Table 5.)

Table 5
Parts of an Article Used to Decide to Read an Article

	Chemists n=16	Sociologists n=16	Humanists n=14
Abstract and figures	11	2	
Abstract, introduction and figures	2	6	
Abstract, conclusions and figures	3	3	
Abstract, introduction and conclusion		2	
Abstract and conclusion		3	
Introduction or first few paragraphs			7
First few paragraphs and footnotes			1
Scanning article			6

All chemists make the decision by reading the abstract and looking at the pictures and their captions. In all cases the combination of the abstract and pictures was sufficient to make the decision. The point was made and stressed often that the figures have to include the captions.

> *The captions are essential so that without reading anything of the body of the text, you can look at the figures and understand them. Having enough information in the caption is certainly very important.*

Chemists expressed the opinion that if the combination of the abstract and figures is not adequate for making a decision, the next level should be the whole article.

While the abstract was mentioned as often as the figures, the chemists appeared to have stronger feelings toward the value of the figures in their decision-making. Some typical remarks were:

> *To me the figures are the most important, and after that the abstract. I think that's peculiar to chemistry.*

> *If there are any graphics that are especially interesting, I focus on these, and then I guess I go back and read the abstract.*

> *The graphics are really of critical importance.*

> *The abstract, the way they're written, tends to be a mish-mash.*

The sociologists were unanimous in their choice of the abstract as one part of the article they require to help them decide whether or not to read the entire article. The part of the article which ranked second was the figures, identified by 75 percent of the sociologists interviewed. Beyond that 50 percent indicated that they use the introduction and 50 percent use the conclusions.

If sociologists were provided with the abstract, figures, introduction, and conclusions of an article, all would be satisfied. If just the abstract and figures were to be provided, as for chemists, only two sociologists would find that adequate. Apparently the abstract in sociology journals needs additional enhancement such as the information found in the introduction or the conclusions. Some typical statements were:

> *You can't totally trust the abstract.*

> *There is too much variation in the abstract.*

> *You can't really rely on the abstract.*

> *Abstracts vary a lot. But in terms of letting me know whether I would like to get into it further, yes, I think they're often reliable. But I read the conclusion which is more useful. The*

> *reason I think the conclusion is important is because there is a lot of variance in terms of where the authors put down what they are really up to.*

> *Well, the abstracts are often not very satisfactory because they're so brief and terse, but one does look at the abstracts just simply to see whether or not it's worth any pursuit. You get most information from the discussion and from the introduction.*

The humanists presented a different case. For the most part the articles they read are not structured into the traditional parts found in science articles. On occasion, however, an abstract is provided. In deciding to read an article the scholars were fairly evenly divided between choosing the first few paragraphs for the exposition of the problem, and scanning the entire article, even when an abstract is available.

> *I would much rather scan than look at an abstract.*

In fact, all scholars remarked that the use of parts of an article to decide whether to read an article is accompanied by skimming or scanning the article. They were quite reluctant to forgo the scanning since the author and title provide inadequate information, the abstract of an article is useful but flawed, and there would be the significant loss of serendipity.

> *If the abstract were the only mechanism, it would be a problem because I would be limited by what the authors had chosen to put in their abstract and then I would be really concerned that there might be something in an article I wouldn't get that way. I want to look at the journal page by page.*
>
> *— Chemist*

Scholars were next asked the question, "Having decided to read an article, do you read the entire article?" (See Table 6.)

The chemists do not read the entire article; the sociologists are more inclined than chemists to read the entire article, and the humanists more often than not read the entire article. However,

Table 6
Procedures Used When Reading an Article

	Chemists n=16	Sociologists n=16	Humanists n=14
Reads entire article		11	11
Does not read entire article	16	5	3
Reads in sequence		9	12
Does not read in sequence	16	7	2

those who do not read the entire article made the point that if the article was extremely relevant to their work, they would indeed read it all very carefully and more than once. These instances are few.

> *I don't have time to read the entire article in detail UNLESS it's something I'm intensely interested in or it somehow obviously overlaps my work, and that will make me interested.*
> *– Chemist*

> *I seldom read an article in a journal the way I read articles when I review them, that is carefully and critically.*
> *– Sociologist*

Scholars were asked whether, after deciding to read an article, they read it in the sequence in which it is written. The chemists, without exception, do not read in sequence. Half the sociologists and almost all the humanists read in sequence.

Scholars were asked to identify which time span of journals tends to be the most useful to their academic work. They were not provided with specific time spans to choose from. (See Table 7.)

In the case of the chemists, most physical and organic chemists need journal literature from as long ago as twenty-five years or all the way back to the beginning of publication. The others use the last fifteen years, with the shortest time span

	Chemists n=16	Sociologists n=16	Humanists n=14
Table 7			
Most Useful Time-Span of Journal Literature			
last 5 years	1	3	1
last 10 years	7	3	2
last 15 years	1	3	2
last 20 years		3	
last 25 years	2	1	
all years	5	3	9

mentioned by any chemist being five years. Some chemists selecting the lengthy time spans suggested that this was not the case for
their use of all journals, but for the most prominent in their
field.

> When I'm doing more on the experimental side, looking for
> specific information, that can go back a long, long time. If
> it has to do with preparative organic chemistry, it can go
> back to the beginning of time.
>
> — Organic Chemist

> There are many things that were generated let's say more
> than 20 years ago, which are still very, very useful. But be-
> yond maybe 25 years, we don't use it very much.
>
> — Physical Chemist

> To me the most important are the last five years. Five to ten.
> 90% of the references I use would be within the last 10 years,
> the last 5 years. So I guess overall I would opt for the last 10
> years.
>
> — Theoretical Chemist

In the case of the sociologists, those who use the complete time span of journal literature are only those concerned with the sociology of work. The others felt that sociology has changed so dramatically that anything older than twenty years is "junk." They also made the point that they depend on anthologies and books to have reprinted the older, classic material.

Most sociologists drew a distinction between their use of journal literature for teaching and their use of it for research, indicating that they use the most recent three to five years for teaching.

> *If I am interested in what's been done or what's known about a topic, I want to go back farther. True, you start with the most recent, but I like to go back through. That's not typical if you are preparing for an undergraduate course. If it doesn't have a date on it saying 1988, most undergraduates don't read it.*

The humanists presented a different profile. The majority of them stated that the full time span of journals is used in their academic work.

> *I think the articles that appeared in the 1930s in journals like* American Literature *are more often useful to me than the articles that appear more recently because this was the generation in which scholars, for the first time, devoted themselves with some assiduity to ascertaining the facts about nineteenth-century literature. The richest resources are probably between 1930 and 1945.*

> *I think in my field a lot of it is very old stuff. Often you have to go back a hundred years to find things—a small thing somewhere that was published in a journal and has never been published since.*

Even in those cases where the scholar identified a shorter time span, such as ten years, it was qualified.

> *Oh well, I prefer to use the literature back to the beginning, but I think generally speaking, the past 10 to 15 years usually is good enough.*

Table 8
Practices Used With Journal Articles

	Chemists n=16	Sociologists n=16	Humanists n=14
Photocopies important articles	16	16	10
Creates a file of journal articles	15	15	10
Annotates article or underlines an article	12	7	10
Creates a notes file	3	7	5
Spreads out many articles at once when writing	3	1	1

Finally, scholars were asked to identify what they do with the information in an article as they are reading it, and after they have read it. There is a uniform pattern of behavior; scholars photocopy important articles, they annotate and underline articles, and they maintain a file of articles arranged most often by topic. (See Table 8.)

—— Notes ——

1. A. J. Meadows, ed., *The Scientific Journal* (London: Aslib, 1979), 9.
2. Herbert C. Morton and Anne Jamieson Price, *The ACLS Survey of Scholars: The Final Report of Views on Publications, Computers, and Libraries* (Washington, DC: Office of Scholarly Communication and Technology, American Council of Learned Societies, 1986); Annette Simpson, "Academic Journal Usage," *British Journal of Academic Librarianship* 3 (1) (1988): 25–36; D. J. Pullinger, "Attitudes to Traditional Journal Procedures," *Electronic Publishing Review* 3(3) (1983): 213–22.
3. William D. Garvey, *Communication: The Essence of Science* (New York: Pergamon Press, 1979), ix.
4. Meadows, *Scientific Journal.*
5. Garvey, *Communication*, 300.
6. Garvey, *Communication*, 298.

4

THE SCHOLARS' REQUIREMENTS OF AN ELECTRONIC JOURNAL SYSTEM

T he success of a computer-based system of journals will depend on its ability to overcome user resistance; in this case, such a system can be successful only if it can overcome the reluctance of scholars to use a computer-based system of journal literature in place of printed journals. User resistance has been a primary reason in the failure of computer-based information systems.[1] Users refuse to accept the system, and their behaviors range from sabotage of the system,[2] to simply not using it.[3]

The most common causes of resistance are reviewed in a paper by Hirschheim and Newman.[4] They can be summarized as the user's innate conservatism, or preference for the status quo; the lack of a felt need; uncertainty, or some form of fear of the system; or the system's poor interface, providing neither the desirable functions, nor a cognitive mode which matches the mental model and cognitive style of the users.

The scholars interviewed in this study did not seem bound by an innate conservatism, or the compulsion to maintain the status quo. They were accepting of the concept of the electronic journal and acknowledged the movements in the publishing world toward electronic publishing. Every scholar was able to identify advantages that an electronic journal would have over print. There was one reservation, however, expressed to some extent by sociologists, but more emphatically by humanists:

> *Just get it. I feel very strongly, very positively that the advantages so far outweigh the disadvantages that it would improve life vastly. If I were talking about books, that would*

be one thing, but journal articles out of scholarly journals, that would be o.k.

— Humanist

The felt need for such a system is strong. The participants in this study mentioned many times the overwhelming difficulty of keeping abreast of the literature of their discipline. This is bound up both with the sheer volume of it, and the inconvenience of getting to it. They felt that a computerized system of journals has the potential to solve the problem.

Scholars did, however, express uncertainty or fears about the system. They were heavily concerned with the system's functional capabilities, to the point of declaring that unless the system could provide appropriate capabilities it would prove to be a "disaster." This conforms with conclusions drawn from Garvey's studies which indicate that the use of journal literature by scholars is their most important means of formal communication, and unless innovation in the system is compatible with the goals of the individual and aggregate community of scholars, avoidance of the system will result.[5]

Overall, the scholars interviewed for this study generally did not indicate reluctance to accept the concept of the electric journal. All scholars readily identified the advantages it would have over print and did not seem concerned that it would disrupt their work habits.

In the world of information systems design, building an electronic journal system is perceived as building another information retrieval system; scholars use journals to find and retrieve specified information. Therefore, designing a successful system depends on identifying accurately the information scholars will want the computer to retrieve.

However, data from this study underscore the concept that the use of journals by scholars is not simply an information retrieval task. Journals are not just an information dissemination facility requiring only the typical information retrieval processes for their use. Journal literature is a communication mode; it functions as a stimulus to creative thinking, and as a medium for education. These processes do not happen through the traditional information retrieval activity precisely defining the information needed and rapidly extracting it. Rather, the processes of thinking and learning depend on being provided with certain circumstances which will support reading and comprehension.

Stated differently, the computer system will have to accommodate the ways in which users interact with the literature and select what they want. It is crucial to acknowledge that this cannot be accomplished with a typical information retrieval system which is designed for efficient retrieval of precisely defined information. For a computer system to support the functions of journal literature for scholars, it will often have to operate when it is more useful not to prescribe which information should be retrieved. This challenge is well illustrated by the following remarks:

> *I read things that seem most interesting to me, partly just to fertilize my own way of writing and to see what other folks are doing.*

> *Print provides the opportunity to browse, which I could not with the computer, to bring up whatever it is I want. I don't have to know. Not when I browse. I'm looking for an adventure of some sort.*

> *It seems to me that the computer technology is based on the assumption that all our choices and processes are rational and predetermined. Whereas, certainly in my areas of activity, a great deal of mental work is wayward and unpredictable.*

The requirements which have emerged as important to users of electronic journals are presented from two perspectives. First, the requirements have been identified based on attributes of the printed form of journal literature which scholars endorse as so intrinsic to scholarship that they should be emulated by the computer-based system. Second, the requirements reflect the functions which scholars expect because the journals are in an electronic system rather than in print.

A major reason for conducting interviews with scholars from the physical sciences, social sciences, and humanities was to assess whether there are sufficient differences in the way they use journal literature that a discipline-biased interface to the computer system would need to be designed. It appears that the chemists require a greater scope of capabilities in the interface than the sociologists or humanists, but that a subset of that scope could meet the needs of the sociologists and humanists. In short, one interface is feasible.

—— The Indispensable Attributes of Print ——

The journal, as communication between scholars, is a medium of written language, and a tool for organizing complicated thinking.

Comprehension and use of this kind of factual information are dependent upon the way in which the information is encoded. In the chapter "Criterion for Designing Written Information," in the book *Processing of Visible Language* (1980), Wright observes that comprehension is affected by the legibility of the text, its layout, and its language. She summarizes the research supporting these observations and concludes:

> *Clearly a considerable number of presentation factors must be borne in mind, when designing text.*[6]

This body of research has had considerable significance for the presentation of journal literature in print form, and should have significance for its presentation in electronic form. In the same way as the printed text on paper has been honed over the centuries to achieve usability, so will the electronic text have to be designed and presented to allow users to achieve their objectives in using the material. As Wright remarks:

> *The analysis of usability has suggested that written materials are used more easily if they are designed to be compatible with the perceptual strategies, the conceptual knowledge, and the information processing resources of the user. The problem is how to achieve such design, how to convince producers of written materials to consider in detail the usability of these materials.*[7]

This problem can be restated as that of finding the most effective way to present written discourse. Jonassen calls this "the technology of text" in his book *The Technology of Text* (1982). He defines it as *the technology of sequencing, structuring, designing and laying-out of the printed page, whether the text is reproduced on paper or in electronic signals on a cathode ray tube.*[8]

He maintains, consistent with the premise of the present study, that hard copy print cannot survive long as the primary medium for information storage. He acknowledges that reproducing high-resolution images on a TV screen via the human-computer interface poses significant problems for designers since the importance of the structure and presentation of the text to the reader's comprehension is undeniable .

Another author, Charles Hulme, in a collection of edited chapters, addresses the need for those designing and implementing computer systems to be aware of the sorts of processes involved in reading.[9] His chapter, "Reading: Extracting Information from Printed and Electronically Presented Text," summarizes the human reading process and moves into a discussion of the special problems associated with reading from computer screen displays. The electronic form of journal literature will be detrimental to the scholar's academic work unless the technology is designed to accommodate not only the physical tasks but also the intellectual processes inherent to the conduct of that work.

The attributes of print cannot be dismissed as simply something to which the reader is accustomed. The scholars in this study were certainly forthright and consistent in identifying these attributes as crucial to thinking, comprehension, and retention of concepts.

Graphics

The issue of graphics was mentioned strongly by all the chemists, and half the sociologists. There were three primary concerns. The first was that the system should provide the ability to view the graphics along with the text. Up to this point in the development of full-text information systems, the graphics (graphs, tables, chemical structure drawings, illustrations) have not been included because of the technical difficulty of storing them in the same electronic form as the text. Chemists reading an electronic journal have the text displayed on the screen, but the graphics are missing. Given the tremendous importance of the graphics to the text, this is a non-viable system.

> *Graphics is all important and the print is definitely better in that area.*

> *The disadvantage of the electronic system is not having graphics.*

> *The thing that I and other people look at very carefully is the pictures, and if the pictures were missing, that would be reason enough to forget the whole thing.*

The second concern related to the quality of the presentation of the graphics.

> *The electronic journal has to have some minimal quality associated with it. The quality of the figures matters a lot to me. The journal has to be good enough to do that.*

The third area stressed many times was the need to be able to browse on graphics, and to search and retrieve on partial and full chemical structures.

> *You know, anything that contains a four-membered ring or something like that, I would fight to the death for.*

Ergonomics

> *I have bifocals and I have noticed that in operating the keyboard you can't do things with the keyboard. It creates more work going back and forth, because I have to visualize keys, and visualize what's on the screen. It's very wearing.*

> *I'm not crazy about spending hours in front of a computer screen. After a few hours I tend to feel rather in outer space in a way that reading the printed word does not do.*

> *One of the pleasures of print is that I can sit in this chair, which leans back nicely, and read with my feet up, for an*

hour, and then move over to this couch. I can move from one place to another. I don't get tired that way. I rise from the computer screen not really refreshed. I think it is tiring.

Eye strain is very important.

I don't like to read on a screen. When I write my own work on the computer, I immediately have to print it out. I worked in journalism and publishing companies for a number of years and copy edited material on the screen. I hated it. I missed a lot and it was very difficult. I know that you have to have things proof read by 4 or 5 different people to catch as much as one person proofreading a print copy.

You get tired, you get physically tired. I don't like reading microfiche or computer screens. I will do anything to get around it.

Reading on the screen is a serious disadvantage of the electronic system. Moving around to read is necessary. I am not a stationary person.

Here the primary concerns were with the physical discomfort of reading from a screen, and with the fatigue of sitting in a fixed position to read. The unanimous solution was to print anything which seems relevant.

There are several research studies which support the opinion of the scholars that reading from a computer screen is fatiguing. For example, Wilkinson and Robinshaw have reported significantly higher fatigue when reading from a computer screen than reading from print on paper.[10] The monitors used in the study were typical of the type used by many scholars. Their results showed performance degradation within a fifty-minute task leading them to conclude that reading for longer than ten minutes is likely to lead to greater fatigue.

However, the work of Gould, et al. encourages readers to believe that fatiguing effects are not produced if the monitors are of good quality.[11] Based on these two studies, Dillon et al. conclude that

> *users do not find reading from monitors intrinsically fatiguing, but that performance levels may be more difficult to sustain over time when reading from average quality screens.*[12]

They also point out the significant fact that

> *the type of task performed in many of these studies represents a very limited subset of what is labelled 'reading.' Browsing, light reading and formal studying are probably more frequent interactions with written material.*[13]

The point of concern is that reading scholarly text on a computer screen causes considerable fatigue and loss of performance for the reader.

Flipping Pages and Scanning

This is a reading strategy, not simply a means for locating information. The purpose of this style of reading is to gain a sense of a whole context. Sometimes this reading is contained within narrow parameters such as within one article, where scholars need to jump back and forth through the text. Sometimes the context is much larger such as a journal issue containing many articles, where the reader is gathering a sense of the questions being asked and answered, the field of authors represented, and the sequence of the texts.

Many of the scholars interviewed emphasized over and over the importance of this reading process, and stated that scrolling on a screen does not support this mode of reading and information processing.

> *It's harder to skim electronic pages. It would be harder just to look around. I visually have a hard time with things whizzing by me on the screen.*
>
> *I would have to print it out. I cannot flip backwards and forwards between different pages.*
>
> *You can't reread, which is pretty important. Computer screens don't look the same. Scrolling back to find something*

is irritating to me—it's the lack of being able to move back and forth.

For me the computer screen is a more limited medium than the printed page. I can jump 3 or 4 pages at a time with my eye going down just to see if anything hits. Scrolling is a much more methodical thing and also, as the page itself moves, you can't focus on it. You have to stop it. One talks about the freedom of the electronic medium, but it is a lot more limiting in terms of how the mind can handle it.

That feeling that you are always cut off from it in some way and scrolling back and forth doesn't quite do it. That is a major problem I have with it.

Theoretically, you can scroll it up and down, but it is much more—you don't have the same access to the whole thing.

One limitation I find when I'm dealing with a document that I've written and it's many pages, is getting from one part of it to the other. In a journal or written copy, what I do is look over here, and I look over there. People run into difficulty with trying to look at long documents on the screen.

It is important to see the whole page—you get a better feel for the information. Certainly, the ability to flip back and forth comfortably is an advantage of the print.

In essence, scholars are stressing the difficulty when they lose a mental model of the whole context with which they are involved. This leads to a degradation in navigational ability and comprehension. They seem convinced that scrolling on a computer screen is not an adequate technique to support the intellectual needs at work when flipping pages of journal text.

There has been some research on the relative merits of paging and scrolling. The evidence suggests that readers establish a visual memory of the location of items on a page and within a document.[14] Scrolling weakens these relationships.

Some of the participants interviewed expressed a sense that another important element in the flipping and scanning process is the tactile sensation—the sense of touch and control of the pages.

> Chemist: *I think there are real things and intangible things, I don't know enough about the psychology of things, but I think there's something about the combination of tactile and visual scanning that makes them more efficient.*

> Question: *You used the word "tactile"?*

> Chemist: *Well that's what I'm doing with my fingers. The scanning process involves a combination of feeling and seeing, of tangible control and seeing.*

Tactile is defined as: "Depending on the sense of touch (as for orientation) . . . fingers as antennas" (*Webster's Third New International Dictionary*, Unabridged. 1971.) This definition of tactile could be restated as the sense of controlling the journal pages with the hands. The tactile aspect of the print format was very important to 75 percent of the chemists at Penn and 75 percent at Cornell.

The dependence on a mental model of a whole context was raised as intrinsic to comprehension not only in the scanning form of reading but also in purposeful reading. Even though many scholars do not actually read in a linear fashion, but jump around in a text, their orientation of where in the whole they are reading is still vital.

> *What I am usually doing when I am reading a journal is listening to a fairly complicated argument. For the most part, I am listening to the kind of thesis or argument that the person is making. Something about reading on the screen throws me off. Even when I am writing on the word processor, I will write five pages and run it off because I like to see what I've written in print. There is something totally different sitting there looking at it.*

> *I lose continuity. If I have a stack of papers and I am reading a paragraph, I have a sense of what follows that you*

don't get on the screen. I have a very difficult time under-
standing and comparing, per chapter or per article, when I
am working on the screen.

The physical location of where you are reading within the
whole, how far you are from the subsection break and so on.
This is important.

Serendipity

The serendipitously discovered article is of great importance
to scholars and although there are several circumstances in which
serendipity happens, the two most common are when the scholar
is browsing the recent issues of a selected group of journals, and
when he or she is retrieving a specific article from a journal and
flips through the surrounding articles.

Serendipity is the chance finding of an article on a topic
which would otherwise have been missed in a systematic literature
search. However, serendipity is frequently a more significant turn
of events in the scholar's creative process. In flipping pages, the
scholar's eye makes a chance contact with a phrase or perhaps a
sentence in an author's conclusion, which stimulates a completely
new and unanticipated line of thought. It is this latter form of serendipity which scholars maintain is so vital to their scholarship.

There are really two different mechanisms of information re-
trieval. One is where I have the concept and I want to find
what is written in the literature and the other is the page
flipping process where I don't have the concept. I'm not
looking for anything, I'm just reading the article.

The limitations [of the computerized system of journals] are
that I would read only the articles that I think I want to read.
I wouldn't have read those where I suddenly see a picture and
I say, 'Oh, that looks pretty interesting.' I do that a lot. That's
the biggest fear I have. I can cite numerous cases where I was
xeroxing an article from 1965 and I turn the next page and
there's a better article. That happens all the time. I think the
biggest incidence is in the current literature.

It's a little hard to define or talk about, but there is a kind of serendipity—if you look for one article, you find other articles. I find this very, very important. I think everyone does. The serendipity factor is very important.

Serendipity is very important to me. It is like browsing in the stacks. I can't see how you will be able to computerize that. I'm sure all of my colleagues greatly enjoy that serendipity.

Serendipity occurs because of the structure of printed journal literature and the visualization of a body of text. It occurs through the action of turning pages, something which has to be done in order to get to a specific page where there is a known article of interest. Seeing at least the articles preceding and following cannot be avoided. In the computerized system it is technically possible for the scholar to see the articles on either side of a selected article, but the scholar's actual purpose is to find that one specific article. The computer does this very efficiently and the scholar's purpose is quickly accomplished. Disarmed by success, there is little incentive to look at the articles on either side. It could be hypothesized, then, that given the convenience and efficiencies of the computerized system of journals, the scholar might be willing to forgo serendipity. The question was asked of several scholars, and the answers were all the same.

Question: *Are the convenience and efficiency (of the computerized system) greater, more important than the serendipity which occurs when you look at the pages of a journal?*

Answer: *I don't think it is, and I want both. I would choose serendipity.*

The answer is both. There is no way to make that decision. That is, they are both important and so any change we make has to satisfy both.

The concept of serendipity was not actually posed to the interview participants. It arose spontaneously within the context of answers to other questions. The concept was always articulated in an emphatic tone of voice and was identified as important by 82 percent of the participants, spread fairly evenly amongst the chemists, sociologists, and humanists.

It is important for a systems designer to acknowledge that serendipity is crucial to scholars not because it finds a journal article which was missed by other searching methods, but because it provides conditions which are a significant stimulus to creative thinking. Scholars depend on journal literature for new ideas, and particularly on the unexpected connection of ideas presented by the serendipitous experience.

Searching

The three disciplines showed very different levels of use of computerized searching to find the background literature of a subject. Computerized searching was chosen only by chemists as the primary method for finding background information. It ranked a distant third for the sociologists and was practically never used by the humanists.

This apparent reluctance of the sociologists and humanists to use a computer to conduct literature searches bears scrutiny, given the interest of this present study in the scholars' use of computers to access journals.

Data were reviewed to examine the correlation between the scholars' use of computers generally and their use of computers to search databases of literature citations. The hypothesis was that little or no involvement with computers generally would equate with little or no use of computers to search citation databases.

The profiles of computer use by the chemists and sociologists, however, are very similar. Both groups have access to microcomputers at home and in the office; both groups use microcomputers approximately the same amount of time each week; and both groups work with a similar range of applications beyond word processing. They differ only in the one category of using computers to search databases. In short, the sociologists "computer literacy" seems similar to that of chemists and does not offer a ready explanation for the sociologists' apparent reluctance toward computerized searching. (See Table 9.)

By contrast, humanists rarely have access to a microcomputer in their office. Those scholars who have one at home have bought

	Chemists n=16	Sociologists n=16	Humanists n=14
Table 9. Microcomputer Use by Scholars			
Access to microcomputer	16	16	13
Used at home	11	12	11
Used in the office	15	16	3
Used both places	9	12	
Hours of use per week			
Less than 10	5	2	8
10-20	5	11	5
20-40	5	3	1
More	1		
Applications			
Wordprocessing	16	16	14
Statistical analysis	8	12	
E-Mail	8	10	1
Searching Online catalog	3	4	2
Searching databases of references to literature	13	5	1
Graphics	11	4	

it with personal funds and it tends not to be state-of-the-art. Humanists generally use their microcomputer ten or fewer hours a week and almost exclusively for word processing. These characteristics could help to explain the humanists' non-use of computerized literature searching.

Although some scholars use computerized literature searching, almost all are dissatisfied with it.

The scholars' reservations are worth noting because they provide insight into some of the shortcomings of computer searching. The chemists remarked that it takes too much time.

It requires a student who is willing to figure out the system. It's obviously a desirable function, but I've got so many other things that I'm just not doing that.

In nine out of the twelve instances where chemists mentioned that they use computerized searching to identify retrospective literature, students actually conduct the search.

In addition, chemists expressed their frustration that the indexing of the contents of journal articles allows retrieval of the literature on only the most straightforward concepts and as a consequence,

Subject searching is not very useful.

Computer searches I have not found to be helpful. I certainly have had students try it many times. It has not been helpful in terms of finding things we didn't already know about, or narrowing down the information that I needed. Usually we get so many citations that it's just impossible to sort out what's there.

Sociologists and humanists also feel that computerized searching has serious shortcomings when relied upon to identify the literature of a subject. This limited ability of the computer to search effectively other than in a routine manner (for specific titles, authors, facts, chemical names, etc.) was mentioned many times by interview participants.

In a study of communications and information processing in scientific disciplines, Garvey agrees, and declares that

after years of extensive planning, developing and trying out of rational, discipline-oriented information systems, it is apparent that these systems, which promised much, have largely failed in terms of attracting widespread use.[15]

It is important for systems designers to acknowledge that "a great deal of mental work is wayward, unpredictable," that all choices are not rational and predetermined. As a sociologist remarked,

You really get into ideas and intellectual connections that computers don't make.

Journal literature in electronic form, like journal literature in printed form, has to provide the circumstances which allow the creative stimulus and education functions expected by scholars. Something beyond the typical process of information retrieval is essential. A system is needed which enters the scholar visually into the actual corpus of the literature creating the circumstances which allow the scholar to "rummage around," and carry out the "wayward mental work" and "intellectual connections" which are unique to the individual. The design of the system needs to provide a real-world metaphor.

> *The computer isn't half as good as the human brain, and when I'm scanning something, I often see something that triggers a different response.*
>
> *— Humanist*

> *There's another way you do a search, and you actually begin to make connections in doing the search yourself. I can instruct a computer to do some of that and it will do it faithfully depending on how the program was written, but it still won't do it the way I do it.*
>
> *— Chemist*

> *It must be realized that paper has been, and will be, with us for a long time and electronic presentation will not always be an improvement. We must repeatedly remind ourselves that the user has a job to do, and design the technology to support the task.*
>
> *— Systems Designer*

Underlining and Annotation of the Text

> *I do a lot of underlining. I think it wouldn't be easy to translate the kinds of note taking that I do into the computer and I'm not even sure I would want to. Part of my problem is the machine takes thought from me.*

> *I can scratch with red pen under it more easily than I can highlight passages on a computer.*

Every scholar mentioned the need to annotate and underline articles when reading them. For some this is a method of highlighting important ideas for efficient rereading of the article later. However, it also appears to be an executive control process in reading which assists comprehension and the assimilation of concepts.

In the same way as the tactile element in flipping pages may be important to the scanning style of reading, the tactile element in underlining and annotating concepts may well be important to the more deliberate style of reading.

> *The thing I worry about is the transition to doing a lot of reading in a way that I'm not used to reading, which means having the journal open, having pencil in hand, taking notes on this card. I'll have to do it in a somewhat different way in the electronic form.*

> *What helps me is when I write on the card—that writing process helps me remember what is there. You have to think about it while you write.*

> *Well, I say it's [underlining, making notes] part of reading it [the article] slowly enough to really see what's there. I'd say it's a re-reading tool and clearly, marking in the margin and rewriting into a notebook is for assimilating the concepts.*

One might conclude from these remarks that the physical connection of the hand to the words and control of the page by the hand assists the transmission of the intellectual content on that page to the mind.

In the electronic system, an underlining and annotation mechanism which provides a tactile connection to the words will be an important function. New microcomputers with data input via a pen on the screen are under development in the major computer manufacturing companies and may readily satisfy this need.

Visual Impress, Weight of the Printed Word

> *Having a hard copy of an article as I work on it is essential. The printed version of it is absolutely essential. I think that when we as scientists hear about the electronic journal, we reject it because we think that means we can't have printed copies of it. In order to use it, really it requires the print of it for me.*

The portability of the printed page was certainly one very frequently mentioned reason for wanting a printed version of articles. However, an even more forcefully expressed reason was the intellectual discomfort of reading on a screen. Scholars described several different concepts related to this.

> *I couldn't possibly just read off the screen. For one thing, I lose continuity.*

> *It's more difficult to absorb on a screen. I have to have a hard copy.*

> *I don't like reading on the screen. Whereas the journal that comes to my desk has a fighting chance of having one article read in it, there would be no chance of any article in that issue being read if I had to go and flip the pages of a computer. I find it more eye straining than reading a book. The idea of sitting in front of a screen and reading an entire article is not a good idea.*

> *That feeling that you are always cut off from it in some way. That is a major problem I have with it. But if I can get a printed copy that would be okay. Otherwise, I'm not sure I'd be able to use it efficiently.*

These perceptions by the scholars interviewed in this study are supported by experimental data reported in the literature. A paper by Dillon et al., "Reading from Paper versus Reading from Screen," reviews the literature on the reported nature, and potential causes of, reading differences between paper and screens.[16] The authors identify much the same areas of concern as the scholars in the present study. The research shows several potential deficits for screen reading: speed, accuracy, fatigue, and comprehension.

Some causes for these deficits appear to be the display size for the presentation of the text on the screen, the "manipulation factor" (merits of scrolling versus paging), the input devices (the mouse versus the keyboard), and the design of icons to represent actions.

An area discussed with the scholars in the present study is the appearance of the text on the screen, and the nature of the type fonts used. Two questions were presented to the interview participants:

> *Is it important to you that the different fonts (style of typeface) of the various journals be replicated in the electronic presentation of the journal?*

> *Is the printed volume important to you as an artifact of scholarship?*

To the first question, concerned with the appearance of the font in the electronic journal, all of the chemists but one answered that the type font is not important.

> *As far as I can see, the crucial matter is just the information and being able to read it. I don't care about the style that much.*

> *You mean, the fact that I have been reading* JACS *(*Journal of the American Chemical Society*) for years and I like the style of it? NO! It wouldn't be worth the money.*

However, a concept which emerged strongly once again within the context of the scholars' responses to the question regarding the fonts was the concern that what does matter is the quality of the representation on the screen of the chemical structures along with the quality of reproduction of the printout. These chemical structures are interchangeably called pictures, graphics, or figures.

The second question regarding the importance of physical aspects of the printed journal asked whether the printed volume was an important artifact of scholarship to the chemists. The answer in almost all cases was a ready "no!" There was one exception, however, who expressed quite strong feelings and two chemists who expressed some regret.

While the chemists seemed adamant, the sociologists and humanists were less sure that the appearance and type font of the text are unimportant.

> *I think the font is important in books. In the journal I think it does help to distinguish one article from another, and it may be that the spontaneity of the type face makes it less monotonous to read, but I'm not sure of that. I do think having a difference in paper and type fonts has a lot to do with how you perceive what you read.*
>
> *– Humanist*

> *There are many pleasures in print. For one thing, poetry especially, the appearance of a poem on a page is an aspect of the aesthetic experience, seeing the poem, the shape, the way in which there is an interplay between print and white space.*
>
> *– Humanist*

> *I love reading the* AJS *(American Journal of Sociology). I always like the colors the editors choose. It is a nice, heavy, thick paper and I like that. I think that set of intangibles is very often what determines whether I am going to read something, or not read it; whether, when I read, I am going to pay attention to it, and absorb it or not. So the answer for me is "yes."*
>
> *– Sociologist*

> *I guess I kind of like the feel of books and journals that have different type pages, different styles. I don't know if you could reproduce it on the screen. I'm not sure whether it would seem kind of silly to do that or not. It is something I think is one of the nice things.*
>
> *– Sociologist*

A number of humanists and sociologists during the course of the interview also mentioned another concept related to the appearance of text on the screen. This had to do with the "credibility" and "weight" of the text. These comments add some strength to the idea that the nature of the text on the screen affects reading performance.

What is difficult about having journal literature in electronic form is that it feels fluid, it doesn't feel stable there; and as far as the content, I think I process it as inherently malleable when it comes through in electronic form which is why I like to print it out and read it.

Your word impress is part of it too. I think that reading on the screen is less, it doesn't create the kind of impression, in the good sense, that print does, and it's just the fact that it's light and not there.

Printed literature is culturally syntonic with my notion of what scholarship is. And the other feels depersonalized.

It is a funny thing about print for me. Somehow it is not still. It doesn't go anywhere, but it's not still. Sometimes it's quite noisy. Whereas a monitor for me is absolutely flat. My experience is that it has no dimension. Putting something into the computer is a little different. Something that you have written, felt and managed, that is one thing. But to have to read that way, I don't know about that.

Because it (the computer screen) flickers, and there's just a little bit of light there, and it's not palpable. It is not MY paper there. The concepts need to be tied to the concrete. Concept formation is enhanced the closer you have the real thing.

I have a fear that I don't retain what I read in the machine as well as I retain from printed matter. Perhaps it's an illusion because on the machine it looks like it's there, and then it's gone; whereas in the book you know it's right there.

Research reported in the literature on comprehension when reading text from a screen does not appear to address the effects of "weight" and "visual impress." Various studies investigate the presentation of text on a screen in relationship to the reader's comprehension, but use screen size and splitting of text across paragraphs as the variables.[17] The conclusions generally are that the optimum display issue requires empirical attention. However, recent work by Dillon and McKnight is concerned with how best to present non-linear text (hypertext). Some of the issues and insights can be related to linear computer text:

> *It is clear from the literature cited that researchers from a range of disciplines see the concept of text types as valid. The issue then is to distinguish meaningfully between text in terms suitable for present purposes.* [18]

And in the discussion of their results, Dillon and McKnight state:

> *The results demonstrate that peoples' manner of construing texts is complex and influenced by numerous factors. Clear distinctions between texts such as 'fiction and non-fiction' have been shown to be simplistic and superficial. On a psychological level individuals are more likely to make distinctions in terms of the type of reading strategy that they employ with a text, its relevance to their work or the amount of information that a text contains.* [19]

Clearly the scholars' dissatisfaction with the way text on a screen affects their reading is a legitimate concern.

Browsing

The scholar's purpose in browsing the journal literature is education. As one chemist expressed it when describing browsing:

> *I'm not talking about proposal writing or paper writing, we're talking about education, my education.*

> *I think that is one of the drawbacks of the computerized system—you have to be much more purposeful in going to a computer system than you would be with the printed journals.*

> *If I don't look at, look through, journals the way I do now, I am going to miss a lot. When you only look in the very focussed way of a computer, around one particular topic or task that you have at hand, there's lots you don't see; and the other kind of information settles into your mind and three*

months down the road I'm going to remember I saw this ar-
ticle by so and so on a topic. Maybe I wasn't looking for it
at the time. I often see articles by other people on other topics,
people whose work I'm interested in, topics I'm interested in,
and I'll sit there and look through things. That's the prob-
lem, I look at a lot of different things. I don't think I would
do that with a computer system. It is the accumulation of
knowledge that you get about what is going on with the field
at large that is really important.

The ability to thumb through printed journals, to tell you
whether it's something you want to read or not. If you are
looking at something, or for something, and then you see
other things around it that catch your eye, you need to have
it physically there to do that. Even if, with a computer, you
search in subject areas, that's good for a specific search, but
not if you are trying to keep current with the rest of the dis-
cipline. You get a sense of people with the print, of names,
and you pick up a journal and pretty soon you start to see
that name two or three times, and you feel that it's somebody
potentially important and interesting.

I think browsing is THE most important thing and it's hard
to believe that you could accomplish that any way electron-
ically.

The need to browse is further reinforced by the unsatisfac-
tory nature of a journal's Table of Contents. The interview participants commented many times on the deficiency of the Table of
Contents in providing the reader with a sense of the usefulness of
articles. This was not only mentioned by scholars as a reason they
browse journals, but it was underscored when scholars discussed
the technique of keeping abreast of literature through receiving
copies of the Table of Contents pages from the recent issues of
selected journals.

The conventional wisdom is that this is a quick, easy way to
keep abreast of the literary front in a wide scope of journals without having to subscribe to the individual journals or go to the library to see them. Six scholars mentioned that they use a Table of

Contents service, but an equal number volunteered that they specifically choose not to use a Table of Contents service.

> *Just looking at titles alone is not enough. When I browse in the journals, I don't just look at the Contents page and put the journal back down again. You look at the Contents and flip through.*

> *I thought that [Table of Contents service] was going to be very helpful to me. But I found that it wasn't as satisfying. I just didn't have the sense of what the magazine was or whether the magazine had the type of literature that's going to be helpful to the kind of work that I do.*

This user attitude and behavior do not conform either with the conventional wisdom nor with that described by Dillon et al. in "Human Factors of Journal Usage and Design of Electronic Texts."

> *Firstly, all subjects look at the Table of Contents of the issue. A preference was expressed for contents printed on the front or back page which made location of relevant articles possible without opening the journal. At this point, readers tend to scan the contents by looking primarily at the titles of papers or the authors.*
> *If the reader has failed to identify anything of interest by this point, then the journal is put aside and, depending on the circumstances, furt journals may be accessed and their contents viewed as above. When an article of interest is identified then the reader opens the journal at the start of the relevant paper.*[20]

In an electronic system of journals, the Table of Contents of each issue provided as a means for deciding on which articles to read, would prove inadequate. When scholars were asked which parts of an article beyond the author and title they use to decide on whether or not to read an article, chemists identified the abstract and pictures, sociologists the abstract, pictures, and introductory paragraphs, and humanists, the abstract (when available) and introductory paragraphs.

The Table of Contents for each journal issue needs to be supplemented by the abstract, pictures, and introductory paragraphs of the articles listed in the Table of Contents. This would be a more effective tool in assisting scholars to choose articles to read.

—— Improvements over Print Expected —— of an Electronic System

Access to the Literature

Throughout the interviews, scholars repeatedly mentioned the barrier they feel in access to printed journal literature. This barrier was always characterized as the necessity to leave their office and go somewhere else to get the literature. A short distance seemed to provide as much of a barrier as a long distance. Their keen expectation of electronic journals is that access to them can be right in the office or home, not down the hall or in the library.

> *I would say if you're talking about me being able to push a button and have access to what's in the journals, then the barrier's gone.*

> *I think the biggest thing is that I could have a full set of journals at my house.*

> *One of the things it would do for me would be that it would make a large number of journals accessible very quickly.*

> *But I think the biggest thing is if I could have a full set of journals at my office.*

Furthermore, and just as significantly, scholars expect that the electronic system will provide that critical mass of literature which they typically use. This was stressed in several ways.

> *I think there's going to be a barrier to using this until it's sufficiently comprehensive that I can turn it on and get what I want. Number one factor is coverage of the literature.*
> — *Chemist*

I don't see what principle of selection (of journals for the system) one could rationally use for the kind of thing I do. When are you going to find the particular thing you want? How far back you have to go in the literature does not come into it.

— Humanist

If I were to put down in a paper the references I believe to be pertinent and look at the date, the oldest one might go back just a few years. Then there will be an occasional one that goes way back because I'll have gotten some compound that was prepared in the literature. If I have to go to the library to look up that occasional one, that's perfectly fine because I know it's an immense amount of work to get the older literature into a database. In this whole business of electronic journals, it seems to me the thing which makes perhaps the most sense would be to do a few important ones all the way back.

— Chemist

The key is to decipher what constitutes a critical mass of literature for the electronic system. In an effort to determine this, scholars were asked,

"Which time span of journals is the most useful to you?"

The chemists' responses divided into those from organic chemists who want all journal literature all the way back, and the other sub-disciplines who could be satisfactorily accommodated with ten years of most journals, and all the way back of a selected group.

The sociologists feel the nature of sociology has changed so dramatically in the last twenty years that literature older than twenty years is "junk." They would be satisfied with fifteen years, with the exception of those who study the sociology of work and need the complete literature.

The humanists consistently want the journal literature all the way back. However, those who work with the sub-discipline of 20th century literature would be satisfied with fifteen years.

In attempting to resolve the "critical mass" issue, it should be noted that studies indicate that a core group of journals tends to satisfy a high percentage of needs. For example, a study in 1983 by Haarala indicated that a core group of 200 science serials covered 50 percent of the total use, 80 percent was covered by 534 titles, and 90 percent by 740 titles.[21] An earlier study by Beaver presents much the same data, revealing that 75 percent of the scientific literature used is in 25 percent of the journals.[22] The first quantitative observations of this phenomenon were made by S.C. Bradford, librarian of the Science Museum Library, United Kingdom, in the 1930s.[23] This information, coupled with determining the half-life of each journal may provide a good basis for satisfying a high percentage of scholars' demands for literature in the computerized system. The half-life of a journal is the median age of its articles; that is, one-half of the citations to them occurs before and one-half after that time.

Also included in their expectations of convenient access to the literature was the scholars' insistence on a system which is easy to use, and takes little time to learn. Notably, the most emphatic statements came from the sophisticated computer users.

> *I think the obstacle in using it is that every computer system has its own knowledge. I will give you an example. When I went to Germany I worked on the biggest, fastest main-frame computers that exist today. The first thing I had to do was learn to use it. If not for the great desire to do these calculations with this person, and the great motivation that this presented, there was a huge, huge obstacle. I do not always have a week to learn something new. One of the biggest problems with computers is how much you need to know in order to use them effectively. The question that I face all the time is, I could spend all of my time learning how to use computers more effectively and become a computer jock, or I could do science. That doesn't get my science done.*

The chemist was not expressing a resistance to using a computer, but to investing time in learning something which is only a means to the end, not the end in itself. A computerized journal system is a means to an end, so that users are not motivated to invest time in learning anything but the most straightforward functions.

Searching

Scholars readily recognize and expect that the computer is superb as a means for finding very specific information. They distinguish this quite clearly from "subjective" searching where they feel the computer cannot be programmed adequately to identify the literature they would choose as of optimal value.

Searchability—in some ways. If you're interested in a specific thing that can be easily searched, that would be very useful.

The electronic system would be good for title searches, for molecule searching and then for retrieving those papers where we just want one specific paper. Those would definitely be done better by electronics.

It would be really great to pull up an article that I want. Sometimes I go to the library and skim through some journals and I say, 'This is an article I should read,' but I can't do it right then. Now if I could pull that up on the screen when it was convenient and sit here and read it, that would be fantastic. Or if I'm sitting here thinking of something and I just want to track it down, to be able to go over to the computer and do that would be a real advantage.

For the older articles when I am looking for facts, I can envision using the computer system. But it will never replace for me the idea of skimming through my current issues of JACS or whatever.

The electronic system would provide the ability to look for information quickly.

If you need specific information it's much faster. It can scan all the text to find a piece of data. It would be much faster than my stacks of papers. But there's a problem. The computer isn't half as good as the human brain and when I'm scanning something, I often see something which triggers a different response. The computer looks at one fact, nothing more.

One scholar recounted the following anecdote to illustrate how unlikely he believes it is that the computer will be able to conduct a subjective search satisfactorily.

> *Doctors for a long time thought they knew, could put down very clearly, the reasoning that goes into a diagnostic process. Stanford looked into this, to see if they could put this thinking into a computer program. But the interesting thing that turned up was that the criteria that the doctors thought were important to use in making the diagnosis did not produce that diagnosis from the computer. It was an entirely different set of criteria that were eventually used. The thing that I was impressed with was the lack of ability of people to put down for the computer, how they reason. It turned out to be very complex; that is, a person really doesn't know how a mind works. But you are trying to create a little black box for me.*

He was quick to point out, however, that:

> *The huge advantage would be that if it were available, it would not be my primary way to read journals, but I would definitely get more material because I wouldn't have to drag myself to the library. I would definitely just call many more things up that were referenced in other peoples' work, and have a quick look at them.*

Increased Frequency of Use of Journal Literature

Increased frequency in using journal literature was mentioned by some participants in the study. All identified the ease of looking up specific references and acknowledged that they would do that more readily, but in terms of keeping up with the literature, only the sociologists and humanists indicated that they might do that more frequently. Since chemists already read the literature frequently, this is not surprising. The sociologists and humanists were not fully convinced that in practice they really would read the literature more, but speculated on the possibility.

> *I might even spend more time looking at periodical literature. But it would have to involve the availability of the format*

that is my usual access to periodicals, which is browsing, and I'm not sure exactly how that could be set up on the computer.

I think I would use the literature more often.

It is an enormous labor saving device and you should be able to read a lot more stuff.

I would probably use more literature than I do now. I might decide I was overloaded by that, but I would certainly try it. I think it would be a tremendous contribution to scholarship to be able to sit in your office and access journals.

Reduced Lag Time in Access to Recent Literature

One of the most frequently stated expectations by the scholars of computer-based journal literature is that it will reduce the time-lag between the acceptance of an article and its publication. An electronic journal system would print the publication of an article as soon as the next issue of the journal was due, and would not be as rigid in constraining the number of articles in an issue. The present delay in publishing is considered a serious interference to communication between scholars, particularly by the chemists.

Printed literature is, in some fields, almost out of date by the time it gets into print. In some cases it's too late if you read about it then, so you need to know much more quickly than that. So another possible contribution of electronic journals might be more rapid dissemination of information.

I think an advantage would be more rapid turnaround of information.

It would certainly make me feel that I had more immediate access to what was coming out in my field.

It would be there the instant it was available.

There are also new journals appearing all the time. So you would have access, or you would see that they had appeared, without waiting five years to discover them.

A potential advantage is that it could speed up the writing and delivery process.

Creation of Electronic File of Articles

Every scholar interviewed, without exception, keeps a file of photocopied journal articles. Some scholars arrange their files by author, but most organize them by topic. Some simply put them in a box or file drawer, not arranged in any special way.

Almost without exception all interviewed participants are dissatisfied with their arrangement of, and retrieval from their files. In fact, the most common method of retrieval mentioned does not depend on which filing arrangement is used, but on the scholar's "memory." Most despair of the inefficiency of their files, the space they require, and the ungainly sight they present as they age.

A few individuals had attempted to create a computerized index to the files, hoping that better retrieval of documents would result. This was not rated as particularly successful either.

Scholars were pleased with the potential of downloading the full text of articles into a personal electronic file. They speculated that the author, title, and abstract would be searchable by key words and, having searched and identified a suitable list of references to articles in their file, they could then view the full text of the articles. These would also carry any underlining and annotations made during the initial reading of the article.

The issue of your own personal electronic literature file— that is a very tempting add-on.

Especially if I could down-load it onto a disk.

If I had the option of downloading articles to a personal file, that's something I would do.

What I would like to do is quickly make a citation of my personal computer file and get down some comments.

Then the other thing would be that you can organize this stuff instead of it sitting in piles where it's inaccessible. Stuff that you have already looked at would be there for you to access.

What would be really wonderful is if the bibliographic information and the abstract could be downloaded easily into a personal computer file of mine and I could edit it. That would be perfect—if I could call up an article, read it and then if I found it useful download it into storage on my machine.

Space Economy

It will shrink the incredible volume of paper.

The disadvantage of print is the tremendous space that journals take. They take far more than books. They keep coming every year. The deterioration is a problem too.

In earlier years I was pleased to contemplate a row of books or articles, but now I find it cumbersome.

Storage space is a problem.

─── **Notes** ───

1. G. Gladden, "Stop the Life-Cycle, I Want to Get Off," *Software Engineering Notes* 7(2) (1982): 35–39; H. Lucas, *Why Information Systems Fail* (New York: Columbia University Press, 1975); K. Lyytinen and R. Hirschheim, "Information Systems Failures: A Survey and Classification of the Empirical Literature," *Oxford Surveys in Information Technology* (1987): 257–309.
2. G. Dickson et al., "Behavioral Reactions to the Introduction of a Management Information System at the U.S. Post Office: Some Empirical Observations," in *Computers and Management*, 2nd ed., ed. D. Sanders (New York: McGraw Hill, 1974).
3. P. Keen, "Information Systems and Organizational Change," *Communications of the ACM* 24(1) (1981): 24–33.
4. R. Hirschheim and M. Newman, "Information Systems and User Resistance: Theory and Practice," *Computer Journal* 31(5) (1988): 398–408.

5. W. D. Garvey, *Communication: The Essence of Science* (New York: Pergamon Press, 1979), 310.
6. P. Wright, "Criterion for Designing Written Information," in *Processing of Visible Language 2*, eds. Paul A. Kolers, Merald E. Wrolstad, and Herman Bouma (New York: Plenum Press, 1980), 185.
7. Ibid., 190.
8. D. H. Jonassen, ed., *The Technology of Text* (Englewood Cliffs, NJ: Educational Technology Publications, 1982), ix.
9. C. Hulme, "Reading: Extracting Information from Printed and Electronically Presented Text," in *Fundamentals of Human-Computer Interaction*, ed. Andrew Monk (New York: Academic Press, 1984), 35–47
10. R. T. Wilkinson and H. W. Robinshaw, "Proof-reading: VDU and Paper Text Compared for Speed, Accuracy and Fatigue," *Behaviour and Information Technology* 6(2) (1987): 125–33.
11. J. D. Gould et al., "Reading from CRT Displays Can Be as Fast as Reading from Paper," *Human Factors* 29 (5) (1987): 497–517.
12. A. Dillon et al., "Reading from Paper Versus Reading from Screen," *Computer Journal* 31(5) (1988): 457–64.
13. Ibid., 460.
14. E. Schwartz, I. Beldie, and S. Pastoor, "A Comparison of Paging and Scrolling for Changing Screen Contents by Inexperienced Users," *Human Factors* 25 (1983): 279–82.
15. Garvey, *Communication*, 127.
16. Dillon, "Reading from Paper."
17. A. Dillon et al., "The Effect of Display Size and Paragraph Splitting on Reading Lengthy Text from Screen," *Behaviour and Information Technology* 9(3) (May/June 1990): 215–27.
18. Andrew Dillon and Cliff McKnight, "Towards a Classification of Text Types: A Repertory Grid Approach," *International Journal of Man-Machine Studies* 33 (1990): 624.
19. Ibid., 631.
20. A. Dillon et al., "Human Factors of Journal Usage and Design of Electronic Texts," *Interacting with Computers* 1(2) (1989): 185.
21. A. Haarala, "Open Access Use of Serial Collections," in *The Future of Serials: Publication, Automation and Management, Proceedings of the Tenth Meeting of International Association of Technological University Libraries, Essen, Federal Republic of Germany*, ed. N. Fjallbrant (Goteborg, Sweden: IATUL, 1983), 179–84.
22. B de B Beaver, *A Statistical Study of Scientific and Technical Journals* (New Haven, CT: Yale University, 1964).
23. S. C. Bradford, "Sources of Information on Specific Subjects," *Engineering* 137 (January 1934): 85–86; S. C. Bradford, *Documentation* (London: Crosby Lockwood, 1953).

5
CONCLUSIONS

The issue at the heart of this study is that while the use of journals in computerized form provides scholars with some advantages over using the printed journals, that same technology can provide disadvantages which militate against the effective use of journal literature, and therefore against the process of scholarship.

The scholars' points of view on what a computerized system of journals needs to do to perform well are presented in Chapter 4. In examining these requirements it seems that all of them are directed toward overcoming one or the other of two broad problems in using the computerized version of journal text.

The first problem is that the selection of literature which is optimal for an individual requires human, not computer recognition. The particular requirements identified by scholars to overcome this problem are as follows:

- browsing graphics to determine the value of an article;
- flipping pages and scanning to provide a mental model of a whole context;
- having tactile connection with what is being read to assist comprehension;
- experiencing serendipity to locate an article which would not have been found otherwise, and to make chance visual connections with an author's phrase or sentence which unpredictably stimulates a new line of thought;
- searching in a non-predetermined manner to gather "outlier" articles on a topic and to generate new ideas;
- browsing to support ongoing education where the boundaries of what is "appropriate" literature are not, and should not be, fixed; and
- participation visually with a wide body of literature.

The second problem is that the scholar's reading of text is negatively affected by its display on the computer screen. The requirements which emerged to address this problem are as follows:

- ergonomic conditions to alleviate eye strain, difficulty with the use of the keyboard and screen by wearers of bi-focal glasses, fatigue of sitting in one position;
- presentation of text on a screen of adequate size and resolution to overcome degradation of reading performance;
- scanning, using some mechanism other than scrolling to support navigation and comprehension;
- combined tactile and visual scanning to provide control in seeing and understanding the pages of an article;
- underlining and annotating text to assist deliberate reading and transmission to the mind of the intellectual content of "the page";
- creation of a printed version of an article to overcome the reader's sense of being "cut off" from the electronic version of the text;
- portability of the text to support the typically nomadic reading patterns of scholars; and
- type fonts and text design which give the text an appearance of "weight" and authority, establish a visual impress on the reader's mind, and support comprehension as well as aesthetic needs where appropriate.

Today, systems designers readily agree that understanding the user's information needs and matching the interface to those needs is the basis for good design. When designing a system, typically they draw on existing analogs to define the model of user needs involved. For example, the use of the electronic form of the text of patents literature or of legal cases could be considered analogous to that of a scholar's use of journal literature. The model of user needs and the capabilities of such systems could therefore be considered "transportable" to a system of journal text. Successful use of the system would then be regarded as the speed with which the user can retrieve information together with the ease of searching the vast corpus of text.

In fact, the systems of computerized journal text which exist today do emulate the capabilities of other full-text systems. Perhaps the most extensive work under way is that being conducted at Cornell University by a collaborative effort of Bellcore (Bell Communications Research), Mann Library (Cornell), the American Chemical Society, and OCLC Online Computer Library Center, Inc.[1] This effort has built a large computerized system of chemistry journal literature and is carrying out studies of user behavior. A number of areas are being explored, but in particular, the design of the human-computer interface. The work would proceed more productively, however, if a comprehensive model of the scholars' interactions with journal literature was available. The investigation is also limited at this time to chemists as the population of users.

Studies at Loughborough University have investigated a number of aspects of developing an electronic journal. These range from scholars' use of printed journals to experiments with readers using text on the screen versus text on paper.[2] The investigators' overall conclusions are that reading from screens can be as fast and accurate as reading from paper, with the quality of the image being the pivotal variable. However, the investigators note that generally the studies do not really simulate the kinds of tasks carried out by users reading journal articles or books; the reading of these kinds of documents raises questions not only of comprehension, but also of manipulation and navigation. In a follow-up study devoted to reader performance specifically with a journal article, the authors assess the effects of screen size and text-splitting on readers' manipulation, comprehension, and subjective impressions.[3] The results indicate that neither variable affects comprehension, but adjusted manipulation levels are significantly higher in small window conditions. However, this is a very limited study since it takes into account the response to using only one journal article.

There are two pertinent studies which have not yet resulted in formal publication. The first is at the University of Technology, Loughborough, Leicestershire, England. The principal investigator is Shackel, a well-known scholar in the field of human-computer interaction studies. The study is concerned with journal structure and tasks, in paper and electronic media. Its purpose is "to study empirically the use of journals in both paper and electronic media, in relation to the user's goals and to design, and to evaluate alternative journal structures with a view to optimizing their use in the electronic format."[4]

Shackel's approach is to study in detail the behavior of readers through observations of readers interacting with current journals. This initial naturalistic approach will be replaced by experimental investigations as knowledge is amassed. With the understanding of the global patterns of reader behavior with paper journals, the influence of the electronic medium and its use will be examined by having readers view the text presented in the same format on the screen as in paper. This is clearly a much wider ranging investigation than the present study in that it examines the very important question of the influence of the electronic medium on the reader's behavior.

Shackel also conducted some earlier work in the project "The BLEND System. Programme for the Study of Some Electronic Journals."[5] The concept of the electronic journal in Shackel's work

> *involves using a computer to aid the normal procedures whereby an article is written, refereed, accepted and "published".*[6]

He explains that the main thrust at the start of the project was to submit papers and gain experiences of the characteristics and processes of an electronic journal in the form of refereed papers.

Shackel's prototype computer system of journals and his research work do provide a valuable infrastructure for the investigation of further questions. As described above, he is now beginning to explore user response questions.

In the world of information systems design, "full-text" is classified as a genre of information systems, and building a system of journal text is viewed as much the same task as building any other full-text system. The present study did not assume that there are analogs in existence from which to devise a model of the scholar's needs when using journal literature. Instead, the definition of user needs, identification of what constitutes successful use of journal literature, and therefore considerations for the design of electronic journals, have been derived from direct conversations with the scholars.

What has emerged is that indeed there are no analogs. Use of journal text is not like the use of any other corpus of text such as corporate records, newspapers, handbooks, technical manuals, or patents. Journal literature is communication between scholars rather than simply a convenient information dissemination facility. It provides the communication of discoveries, methods, theories, and verification of knowledge. It forms the knowledge base from which the education of scholars is drawn and from which new knowledge is generated. The significant and unique characteristic of the relationship between the scholar and the corpus of journal literature is its interactive nature.

In practice, this means that the use of journal literature by scholars is very often not a matter of the scholar setting out to locate definable information. It is frequently a matter of the scholar entering an extensive knowledge environment and casting around "for an intellectual adventure of some sort." What is being sought cannot be defined to a computer; only the mind of the scholar can recognize or "make connections" with the appropriate literature. This "wayward thinking" and unwillingness to be specific about what is needed is claimed by scholars to be central to successful scholarship. It represents the key difference between the way information is sought and found in journal literature and the way it is sought and found by users of other bodies of text.

For example, users of any electronic text system complain about scrolling as the means of scanning and flipping pages. The problem lies with the discomfort of reading text which is moving before the eyes in such a manner, as well as the loss of intellectual orientation within the whole. However, the scholar reading journal text and scrolling experiences not only the discomfort and lack of orientation, but also the loss of the main purpose in flipping and scanning, namely visual involvement with the wider context of surrounding literature. This is crucial to the serendipitous intellectual connections important to scholars' creative thinking. Perhaps the negative effects of scrolling could be alleviated for most full-text use by the provision of high-resolution screens large enough to display one or more full pages. But this does not accommodate the visual and intellectual needs met by the flipping of pages by a scholar. Garvey underscores this:

In fact, we are concerned that without understanding these other aspects it is possible that increased pursuit of mechanized scientific communication could possibly retard scientific progress. The problem is that we know little about the psychological process of scientific creativity and consequently could do damage to it by changing current information-exchange procedures. For example, is it a foregone conclusion that automating the information-search-and-retrieval process will enhance scientific creativity/discovery? From what little we know about the way scientists go about "creating/discovering," it appears that their exploratory, searching behaviour, as they wind their way through the mass of information, is personally selective. One particular item of interest will lead to the specific seeking of another which will in turn influence the selection of only certain other items. Finally, when all the pieces fall into place, there is "discovery." When this happens, and the exploratory-search process is over and all the pieces are put together again in a systematic, rational sequence, it looks so perfectly simple that it possesses an aesthetic quality. But while it is happening, it appears almost a random decision-making process. And, of course, only a relative few of these random walks through the mazes of scientific information produce successful major discoveries, but we would not want to hinder those few which do produce success to facilitate the many which do not.[7]

If journal literature is to be computerized effectively, systems designers are faced with providing some very different system capabilities from those in a typical computerized system of documents. The typical system is designed to retrieve in the most efficient possible way, specific, clearly prescribed pieces of information or documents. Designing a successful computerized system of journals requires that designers acknowledge the uniqueness of the function of these documents in the lives of their users. This shifts the task from designing the "this is the information I want, go get it" system to designing a system which accommodates the "wayward and unpredictable mental work" which scholars maintain is crucial to the intellectual process of scholarship.

It is a temptation to argue that while scholars are able to describe with precision and conviction their needs in using journal literature, these "needs" have been conditioned by years of using the printed version of the journals. The argument could continue that after becoming accustomed to a computerized system of the literature, scholars will be so pleased with its efficiencies and capabilities that their traditional needs will be superseded.

Perhaps some of this will transpire. Nevertheless, the underlying need in using journal literature will remain—to have an official body of literature to serve as a ground for education in the knowledge of a discipline, and as a stimulus for the development of new knowledge. This requires circumstances which promote reading and learning, and creative and analytical thinking, rather than simply locating specific information. If these intellectual processes are recognized, the electronic presentation of journal literature can be honed to support them, just as the presentation of text on paper has been honed to support them.

The implications revolve around designing technology solutions which go beyond simply accommodating the physical tasks of using journal literature. The solutions have to accommodate the scholars' intellectual activities—creative thinking, learning, or analytical thinking. Each of these activities hinges on the exercise of human recognition in selecting the literature to be read, and on being able to read in different ways. These require difficult technological solutions for optimal searching and presentation of text.

The learning which is typical of scholars using journal literature occurs when they are reviewing the body of publishing for an area in which they are about to begin some research. It also occurs when they are concerned with a colleague's description of methods, or presentation of new findings and philosophies. The learning process requires purposeful reading and the scholars interviewed in this study stressed that an important element in such reading is to have a sense of the whole context being read. Sometimes this is a whole article, sometimes a whole journal issue, sometimes a whole aggregate of literature on a topic. Scholars have traditionally achieved orientation in the print medium by flipping pages back and forth, maintaining, in effect, a "view from the bridge." They jump back and forth within the whole context, and they reread without becoming disoriented or losing their intellectual grasp. As already mentioned, scholars stated over and over again their conviction that the scrolling of text on a computer screen does not serve this purpose.

Creative thinking occurs for the scholars when they make unexpected, intellectual connections with existing knowledge, which result in the pursuit of an unpredicted inquiry. This kind of thinking is supported by exploratory or nonpurposeful reading. The scholars emphasized repeatedly the "waywardness" of this reading and thinking process, and their inability and unwillingness to prescribe ahead of time exactly what they want to read or what they are looking for in the literature. This very lack of specificity frequently establishes the circumstances which allow the serendipitous connections to be made. In the print medium, for example, the scholar achieves the circumstances by visually scanning a critical mass of literature in combination with physically turning the pages. The tactile contact with the pages was mentioned as important both to controlling the speed of reading, and to strengthening intellectual connection with the text. Scholars stressed with some passion that text "whizzing by" on a computer screen does not enable the kind of reading and intellectual interplay with the text which stimulate the creative thinking process. They want to be able "to look around" in a large body of text.

Analytical thinking is used particularly when scholars are sorting through literature looking for articles which have some relevance to their areas of interest. While this could appear to be more of a classic information retrieval process than a reading and thinking process, in fact the scholar feels strongly that only the individual mind can identify the most appropriate literature. The participants in these interviews maintained that computers cannot make the most suitable choices, nor for that matter, can other scholars. They hold firm opinions on the lack of efficacy of computer searching. The ambivalence expressed by scholars toward computerized searching is a significant potential failure factor for an electronic system of journals. From the scholars' point of view, the search systems available today are not satisfactory, specifically in the functions which are the most important in an electronic full-text system. Scholars stress the need to introduce their own base of experience and intellectual analysis to selecting the literature, and to exercise their own judgment in what they sort through.

Successful reading and thinking are of course dependent upon comprehension. The interviews in this study substantiated the findings in other studies that there is a relationship between the way text is provided to the reader, and the reader's level of comprehension. Scholars identified several stimuli or characteristics of scholarly text which influence comprehension of the text. These were its visual impress and quality of appearance, its "weight" and stability, having tactile contact with it, the ergonomics involved in reading it including its portability, and as discussed previously, a sense of its whole context. These particular characteristics were singled out because the electronic medium has a negative effect on them, and comprehension of the text is degraded.

As stated earlier, overall, scholars are not reluctant to accept the concept of the electronic journal in place of print. However, they do stress the principle that unless the electronic form serves their purposes it will be "a disaster."

This study set out to identify these purposes. The conclusions are that while scholars may express their purposes as "finding the comprehensive background knowledge on a topic," or "browsing to keep up to date" or "finding articles in my research area," their actual purposes in interacting with the literature are learning, creative thinking, and analytical thinking. This is a crucial distinction because functions such as selecting articles or browsing the latest literature appear to be tasks which a computer can be programmed to perform well, but in practice the computer performs them quickly, but not well.

How, then, can a system of electronic journals and its interface be designed to overcome these circumstances? Although it was not the purpose of this study to answer that question, speculation on some possibilities seems in order.

One possible solution might be to use a real-world metaphor for the design. An interesting system using this kind of technology configuration was developed by Benest et al. at the University of York in England. Their system was based in a library metaphor which closely modelled the mechanisms for conventional searching, acquiring, and reading of paper documents. Their premise was that models which are already known will be easier to use when similarly presented online. The book metaphor in the system provided an open-book presentation, with animated page turning and the functionality that would be provided by a real book. For example, book markers could be inserted in the book, and pages could be annotated with a highlighting pen. Their point of view maintained that:

> *A conventional approach to accessing a document from an electronic library would be to use a complex query language to find the document, and then to use a system of scrolling the text either a line or a screen page at a time in order to view it. This conventional approach imposes a mechanism that causes interference with the task the user is performing, that of searching and browsing for the information required.*[8]

A more sophisticated technology design might be a multimedia system, a combination of interactive video and information retrieval system. With such a system, the user could be visually "enveloped" in the electronic literature in very much the same way as occurs in print. It would allow simulated page flipping, scanning and browsing, jumping back and forth through the text without becoming disoriented, and the occurrence of serendipity. In addition, the important routine searching efficiencies provided by an information retrieval system would be available.

A yet more sophisticated solution lies with a system designed to provide the scholar with a virtual environment. A virtual environment is well illustrated by the following:

> *In a fifth-grade classroom a student intently watches the screen of a color computer monitor. Karen is carefully following the movements of a realistic, three-dimensional, simulated insect as it slowly walks over a gently rolling surface. As she watches the model animal, she hears the magnified sounds its body makes as the legs bend, rise, fall, push through the grass, and find firm placement in the soil. Absorbed in watching the movements of the creature's legs, Karen is working on her class project to find out how different kinds of legged animals move about in the world. She carefully studies the simulated computer graphics insect from a variety of viewpoints, at normal speed and in slow motion, closely noting the footfall sequence. After Karen understands the gait pattern, she writes a program to control the stepping and swinging of the legs and uses an animated set of rigid*

segments and rotary joints to assemble a simplified version of a sort of six-legged graphical robot. Karen reaches into the scene with a gloved hand and places her robot-insect on the simulated grassy surface. As it begins to move its legs, she watches intently to see if her own construction will perform as well as the computer model has.

Karen is working in a virtual environment (VE). It's a computer simulated world consisting of mathematical and software representations of real (or imagined) agents, objects, and processes with a human-computer interface for displaying and interacting with these models. The interface has two parts:

1. *A logical interface that specifies what parameters of the VE and its models can be changed, and when; and*
2. *A physical interface consisting of visual, tactile, and auditory displays for presenting the virtual world to the human participant and a set of sensing devices to monitor the human's actions.*[9]

Much remains to be done with this technology but the capabilities are coming. For example, virtual environment video games recently debuted in London and San Francisco. This is a powerful visualization tool integrating robotics, artificial intelligence, and computer graphics technologies. This technology configuration embodies the very capabilities which are significant to the scholar's use of journal literature and so lacking in the traditional information system design supporting full-text.

Whatever technology configuration is chosen, it has to solve the two basic problems presented at the beginning of this chapter. It has to provide circumstances which allow human cognition in the selection of optimal literature, and it has to support the scholars' visual comfort and reading styles. Unless these problems are solved the processes of learning, and creative and analytical thinking will be crippled.

Building an electronic journal system cannot be viewed as the same kind of task as building the text systems we have experienced thus far in information systems development.

Building a computerized system of journal literature will require a new frame of mind, an imaginative approach, and an unconventional configuration of technology.

It is imperative that as the twenty-first century dawns, the power and capabilities of the computer be exploited in the management of society's knowledge, but not to the detriment of the power and capabilities of the human mind to generate it.

—— Notes ——

1. Michael Lesk, "The CORE Electronic Chemistry Library," in *Proceedings of the Fourteenth Annual International ACM/SIGIR Conference on Research and Development in Information Retrieval,* Chicago, 13–16 Oct. 1991 (New York: Association for Computing Machinery, 1991), 93–112; Jan Olsen, "The Electronic Chemistry Library; the CORE (Chemistry Online Retrieval Experiment) Project at the Albert R. Mann Library, Cornell University," *SLA Chemistry Division Newsletter* 7(1) (Winter/Spring): 5–7; Dennis Egan, "Hypertext for the Electronic Library? CORE Sample Results," *Hypertext '91 Proceedings* (New York: Association for Computing Machinery, 1991).
2. Andrew Dillon et al., "Towards the Development of a Full-Text, Searchable Database: Implications from a Study of Journal Usage," *British Journal of Academic Librarianship* 3(1) (Spring 1988): 37–48; Andrew Dillon et al., "Human Factors of Journal Usage and Design of Electronic Texts," *Interacting with Computers* 1(2) (1989): 183–89; Andrew Dillon et al., "Reading from Paper versus Reading from Screen," *Computer Journal* 31(5) (1988): 457–64.
3. Andrew Dillon et al., "The Effect of Display Size and Paragraph Splitting on Reading Lengthy Text from Screen," *Behaviour and Information Technology* 9(3) (May/June 1990): 215–27.
4. Personal communication with B. Shackel, June 1988.
5. B. Shackel, "The BLEND System. Programme for the Study of Some Electronic Journals," *Ergonomics* 25(4) (1982): 269–84.
6. Ibid., 269.
7. William D. Garvey, *Communication: The Essence of Science* (New York: Pergamon Press, 1979), 93.
8. J. D. Benest et al., "A Humanised Interface to an Electronic Library," in *Human-Computer Interaction - INTERACT '87,* eds. H. Bullinger and B. Shackel (New York: Elsevier Science Publishers, 1987).
9. David Zeltzer, "The Future Is Now: Virtual Environments and Learning," *Technos* 1(1) (Spring 1992): 19–20.

INDEX

Abstracts, 22-23, 52, 60
Access to literature, 53-54, 57-58
American Chemical Society, 2, 19-20, 65
American Society of Agronomy, 2
Annotations, 28, 44-45, 59-60, 64
Anthologies, 27
Articles, 66
    abstracts, 22-23
    annotation, 28, 44-45, 59-60
    conclusions, 23-24
    length, 37
    long-term value, 25-26
    reading, 22-25
    scanning, 22-24, 36-39
    sequences, 25
    time span, 25-26

Beaver, B., 3, 55
Bellcore, 65
Benest, J. D., 71-72
Bibliographies, 17, 19
BLEND system, 66
Bradford, S. C., 55
Browsing, 17-20, 31, 36-39, 44, 50-53, 63, 72
BRS, 2

Chadwyck-Healey, 2
Chemical Abstracts, 20
Chemical Abstracts Online, 19-20
Chemists and chemistry
    behavior study, 65
    browsing, 17-18, 24, 38
    literature searching, 19-20, 41-44
    reading methods, 22-27
    tactile sense, 38

use of computers, 41-43
use of journals, 15-17
Communications, 1, 13-14
Comprehension, 31-32, 37-38, 45-46, 49, 63-65, 71
Computers
    connections, 4, 18-19
    ease of use, 55
    requirements, 31, 63-74
    screen reading, 35-37, 66-67
    searching, 19-20, 41-44, 56-58
    system failures, 29
    use by scholars, 41-43, 69
Concepts, 44-45, 49
Conclusions of study, 63-74
Connections, 4, 21, 43-44, 63, 65
Cornell University, 8, 38, 65
Credibility, 48
Creativity, 4, 30, 44, 67-68
Current awareness, 14-15, 63
    methods, 17-21, 28, 51

Database use, 42
Depersonalizing, 49
Dialog, 2
Dillon, A., 46,52
Displays, 44-50
Downloading, 59-60

Education, 44, 50, 63, 67, 71
Electronic files, 59-60
Electronic journals (e-journal), 1-2
    access, 53-55, 57-58
    acceptance, 30, 63-65
    advantages, 2-3, 30, 53-60, 63-74
    benefits over print, 53-60